# 30 Days to
# Peace and Joy

## A Journey to Transformation in Daily Bites

Robin Perry Braun, M.Psy.

# DEDICATION

I dedicate this book to Pathways and Class 324. You've shown me unconditional love and acceptance and taught me the power of the heart. My life is so much richer from having connected to each of your hearts.

I also dedicate this book to my girls, Sami, Rachel, Victoryah and Isabella. Walking with God and wanting to hear "Well done my good and faithful servant" one day along with desperately wanting abiding peace and joy has led me here. I pray my journey is a legacy to you and your children.

# ACKNOWLEDGMENTS

Thanks to my friends for believing in me and the many teachers, healers and people who have invested in me. I pray the seeds you have sown in my life reap a great reward for you.

# ACKNOWLEDGMENTS

# CONTENTS

# INTRODUCTION

In the past couple of years, I have been hearing more and more people talk about "Quantum Physics" and the "Law of Attraction" as they apply to everyday life. God had already been leading me on a journey to learn more about this principle. He was clearly guiding my steps from every direction and there has been a sense of destiny for me to pursue a deeper understanding of the principles of Quantum Physics as they apply to living a life as a believer in Christ. I was searching for missing puzzle pieces. I have been involved in inner healing and ministry for more than 20 years but saw something missing in people finding lasting freedom and transformation. They would receive some healing or transformation after a session or workshop but days, weeks, months later, they had the same issues once again. I was one of those people. With all my education, knowledge and healing experiences both personal and professional, why was I still struggling in certain areas?

I really began to search hard when I realized I was battling deep depression. How could someone with so many things going for them and having relentlessly pursued their own healing be so deeply depressed? As I read literature, researched online, etc., I realized I had been using most of these principles in ministry for years but they were only taught to me in a scriptural/spiritual context. They were the same truths, but using different lingo, I began to learn a new context in which to apply them and some deeper applications which I felt provided pieces to this healing puzzle. This led me to write *A Believers Guide to the Law of Attraction*. When I wrote this book, I knew it was a lot of information and my concern was that people could not apply the principles without a guide. After much consideration I felt led to write this follow up book which is more structured, palatable and digestible in smaller bites but also requiring some work that intentionally rewires the brain.

It has been my life's pursuit to find the best modalities of healing for the wounds in Christians and anyone. While I have seen many instant healings of physical issues, I have witnessed few truly

1

instantaneous healings of wounded hearts and these seem to occur little by little in relational settings. Since, the wounding occurred in relationships; God tends to bring healing in relational ways.

In my own journey and from observing that of many others, I have discovered missing pieces in many of the modalities I have seen and experienced. I believe that the truths behind The Law of Attraction, which I will correlate to Biblical principles, provide some very significant missing pieces to the transformation of the whole person --body, soul and spirit. As I journey, I am convinced the secret is in the thoughts and feelings as we have 60,000+ thoughts per day. I believe God has given us what we need to change and master these if we will do the work. Peace and joy were not meant to be elusive, they were meant to be normal. After all, we were created in His image and likeness.


If you knew me well then you would know that I never give up hope or belief. My God is pure love. He did not leave us permanently broken, blocked or damaged. There is an answer for everything we just have to find it – he leads us in the direction we look. Sometimes the answers are in uncomfortable packages because He is not religious. Truth does not always appear in the tidy paradigm/box we have invented. I believe he delights in shattering our boxes so we will stop putting limits on Him. Knowing Him is the most important thing to Him. Seeking truth first and then aligning with scripture allows us to break down the walls between people and brings an awareness of how judgmental we really are. If we really all understood and applied scripture, none of us would struggle. I have found truth outside of the safe church paradigms and aligned it with both the nature of God and His word. I encourage you to live your life the same way. Those who do not claim to know God should not have more peace and joy than those who know they are His children…..and yet this often is the case….

# 1
# WHAT TO EXPECT

I n the next 30 days, you will be given a bite a day. What I didn't tell you is that you are eating an elephant.. This is not your typical devotional where you go, "Oh that was really powerful and meaningful" and it impacts you for a minute as you meditate on it for a few minutes, but three hours later its impact is gone. The purpose of this book is a large undertaking. It is designed to shift your thinking in a major way with the goal of eliminating the things that are preventing peace and joy from your life and including some things that will add it to your life. They may be things you don't even realize. If you did you probably would have eliminated or added them before now.

When I wrote, *A Believer's Guide to the Law of Attraction*, I knew it was an elephant and although I made suggestions on how to change your life, I didn't give it in small bites. I knew a certain number of people would take the information and run with it but most of us need small bites and small changes and we do better when someone else is taking us down the path for that to occur. I go to the gym and attend exercise classes led by someone else so I don't have to figure out how to get in shape and motivate myself. We are so busy in so many things that having someone else guide us in doing some things is a welcomed relief. So I felt led to write this book in hopes that people could begin to change their life based on the paradigm I detailed in A Believer's Guide …

So while you will be given small daily bites, you will be asked to do some real work each day. If you really want to change, there is work involved. It requires mindfulness and intention, so make sure you are fully present to each day and lesson and do the work asked with energy and commitment. At the end of 30 days is a guide to morning and evening suggested exercises. This will help to make a habit of your regular day's processing. You may start before 30 days but the exercises are based on the cumulative knowledge imparted over the 30 days.

# 2
# WHY WE NEED PEACE AND JOY

Ir we are going to reach for something we should probably
better define what we trying to achieve. **Peace** is the absence
of something. It is the absence of fear, worry, anxiety and
other negative energies that make your body and brain race and
malfunction. Its absence allows for focus, rest, connection to
people and God.

**Joy** is not necessarily happiness. It is the result of feeling
connected to self, others and God in a positive way and feels like
acceptance and love. It is not dependent upon circumstances.

*"Joy is the settled assurance that God is in control of all the
details of my life, the quiet confidence that ultimately
everything is going to be alright, and the determined choice
to praise God in every situation"* **- Kay Warren[i]**

Why are peace and joy so important? You might say, "I really
haven't had a life of peace and joy but I'm surviving just fine."
Most people won't admit they don't live in peace and joy. In fact,
most people don't truly value peace. They are accustomed to
chaos and adrenalin and this keeps them moving. We are an
addicted society and peace and addiction don't align well. When I
test peoples bodies, most people have significant imbalances in
their bodies and are not thriving physically spiritually or
emotionally. We live from high to high as a substitute for peace
and joy. But again, the brain is not synchronized when it is not in
a state of peace and joy and neither is the heart. Many people
don't know what this synchronization would feel like, even those
who love the Lord and are committed to living their life for Him.

I am going to give you four big and seemingly selfish reasons why

4

you need to be at peace and joy.

1.  God wired us for peace and joy. Our brains were actually created to stay at peace and joy. They are hard wired for this. Dr. Allan Score[ii], a neurobiologist established this fact based on the activity of the brain. Freud called this brain activity, "The pleasure principle" He said we are driven to a state of pleasure. We call this brain state homeostasis. So our brain is driven to stay at homeostasis. It drives us towards behaviors that will attempt at returning the brain to this state. Dr. Schore explains this in neurobiological terms. All addictive, obsessive and compulsive behaviors are the brain's attempts at homeostasis or returning to peace and joy.

    The problem is that these behaviors are not really authentic ways to achieve this state so they don't work for very long. Anyone struggling with obsession, compulsion or addiction (a combination of obsession and compulsion) is being controlled by their brain's attempts at finding peace and joy in inauthentic ways and it often damages or destroys their life and the lives of their loved ones. Most people's lives who fit this struggle would tell you that their life is not working. So reason one why you need to find peace and joy is that it is the way you were made. Your life just works the way it was meant to work when we are at peace and joy because we are not driven by our obsessions and compulsions.

2.  ***Romans 14:17 -18:*** *"17 The kingdom of God is not a matter of [getting the] food and drink [one likes], but instead it is righteousness (that state which makes a person acceptable to God) and [heart] peace and joy in the Holy Spirit. [18] He who serves Christ in this way is* **acceptable** *and* **pleasing** *to God and is* **approved** *by men."*

So the way to serve Christ is from a state of peace and joy.....period....in this state we are pleasing to God and man. Another translation says we *"have the favor of man."* I sure want favor....don't you?

Those of us who have a heart to really serve God want to "see His Kingdom". We mistakenly think His Kingdom is some kind of place when, in fact, it is a state of being or as we will learn, a frequency. Luke 17:21 says, "The Kingdom of God is within you." We are most effective to the world in this state and we have the favor we crave. Favor is a good thing, it reminds us we are children of a loving God who considers us righteous (Jesus covers all our flaws, mistakes, bad decisions, a.k.a. sin). We have more time and energy to serve God when we have favor.

3. The third reason we should make peace and joy our priority is best understood by using the idiom "above the snake line" Anyone who lives in a higher altitude or is a mountain-goer knows that snakes cannot live at high altitudes. There is a "line" where a snake will stop as it senses changes in the atmospheric conditions related to altitude. Snakes represent forces of darkness of some sort. These entities vibrate at a low frequency.

   When we vibrate at a high frequency of peace and joy, we repel low frequency things in our life, they don't "stick" anywhere. You will better understand this after 30 days. So reaching peace and joy and making it a priority to stay there will safeguard against demonic attacks. Imagine feeling safe from demonic sabotage, attack and loss because you are living "above the snake line" vibrationally.

4. My motivation for making peace and joy my priority occurred a couple years back when I had finished grad school and had no viable source of income. I was worried.

6

I had bought into the Law of Attraction and the connection between Romans 14:17 and Matthew 6:33 ("Seek first the kingdom and all these things will be added" – "these things" refer to provision from Matt 6:30-32). I knew that if I could eliminate worry from my life (a form of fear) I would attract abundance and provision. So quite frankly, I sought out releasing worry from my life as a way to ensure I would not be poor.

So four good reasons to make peace and joy the most important thing in your life are: 1. It's the way you are wired; 2. You will get to dwell in God's Kingdom and have favor; and 3. You are not a target of demonic attacks. 4. You will always have provision and potentially abundance.

# 3
# FOUNDATIONAL SCIENCE
## DAYS 1-5

### *Day 1 - Quantum Physics principle # 1*
### *We are made up of Energy*

***1 John 1:5*** *says:* *"God is light and in Him there is no darkness..."*

Did you know that everything is made up of atoms, tiny particles that are completely comprised of energy particles that are held together by light. We are mostly empty space (not a blonde joke), made up of particles held together by light.

If God is light and, according to *Genesis 1:26*, we are made in His image and likeness, then it would follow that our spirit is made up of the same energy component as God. This does not mean we are actual gods, but the idea that the Holy Spirit could dwell within us makes sense if we truly understand that we are made up of energy. We are made in His likeness....light.

*1 Thessalonians 5:23* says that we are a spirit-being with a soul, housed in a body. If our primary substance is light (spirit) then what we see with our natural eyes (body) is just a hologram of what the real essence of a person truly is.

As we explore the application of Quantum Physics to ourselves in light of God's truths, some amazing revelations will happen that can bring transformation to your life. Be open to looking at your life in some new ways. This will bring you to a new place of peace and joy that you didn't realize was possible. Everything will make sense both scientifically and scripturally in applications that may bring new ways of thinking to you.

***Thought for the Day:*** What does it mean for me to be made up of energy and be primarily a spirit being? How do I wrap my brain around this idea? Journal this idea that we are made up of energy and so is everything around us. Let your imagination freely think about what it means for everything to be in motion and just energy. You can use your own journal or write below. More writing space is available in the back of the book. You can also use a separate journal if you plan to loan out this book.

_____

_____

_____

_____

_____

_____

_____

_____

_____

_____

_____

_____

_____

_____

_____

_____

_____

_____

_____

_____

_____

_____

_____

_____

_____

_____

# Day 2 - Quantum Physics principle # 1
## We are made up of Energy

*John 4:34 says, "God is a Spirit (a spiritual Being) and those who worship Him must worship Him in spirit and in truth. (Reality)*

We are made up of energy. Energy has no mass so why don't we walk through walls? Our atoms in motion make us seem like solids. However we can sense the presence of energy. The Spirit of God has a presence, you feel it. It is not an emotion but you may experience emotion in response to God's presence.

Worship is connection. If we are energy and God is energy, then we connect to him energetically. Our spirit (energy) connects to His Spirit (energy). So why don't we always feel his presence? That is a mystery.

A big part of applying the Law of Attraction (LOA) to your life is to begin to make the quantum leap to seeing the world differently. In the movie, The Matrix, Neo has a revelation that the Matrix is just a computer program and not true reality and learns to use his mind to move matter and himself. The thought life of a powerful Law of Attraction Christian demonstrates this scripture;

*Hebrew 11: 11 "Now faith is the assurance (the confirmation, [a] the title deed) of the things [we] hope for, being the proof of things [we] do not see and the conviction of their reality [faith perceiving as real fact what is not revealed to the senses]"...*

When we live in our spirit, we see life differently and the power of belief/faith begins to manifest things. Few Christians achieve this realization like Neo. Those that do live a powerful, supernatural life.

***Thought for the day:*** Have you ever thought that your mind has that much power? What if that was true? What would you do differently? Write in your journal what would be different in your life if you could make anything you focused your thought upon come to pass. What kind of things would you focus on? What if everything you focused on came to pass? What things would you stop thinking about or focusing on? Be specific based on the things currently going on in your life.

_____

_____

_____

_____

_____

_____

_____

_____

_____

_____

_____

_____

_____

_____

_____

_____

_____

_____

_____

_____

_____

_____

_____

_____

_____

_____

## Day 3 - Quantum Physics principle # 2
## All energy vibrates on a frequency. Different things have different frequencies.

We know that sound waves have different frequencies. When we turn on a radio and tune our FM station to somewhere between 88 and 107, we find precise points where we get a signal and our preferred (or our kids preferred) sounds emitting.

Everything that exists gives off a frequency, not just sound. Even inanimate objects have a frequency. Technology has given us ways to measure frequency. According to the work of Dr. Robert Becker:[iii]

o       The frequency of a Healthy Body is 62-78 MHz
o       Disease sets in at 59 MHz
o       Cold and Flu symptoms begin at 58 MHz
o       Epstein Bar 52 MHz
o       Cancer 42 MHz


Everything we think, say, eat, touch and surround ourselves with has a frequency. You have heard the saying, "garbage in, garbage out". When we are surrounded by low-vibration things and put them in our body, our vibration lowers. The reverse is also true. We will talk about these applications in depth throughout this journey. There are many scriptures that talk about this concept. Most refer to thoughts, words and behaviors. One of the scriptures we will talk about and elaborate upon repeatedly is *Proverbs 23:7: "As a man thinks in his heart so is he."* You are what you think… This includes feelings, emotions and words-they are all interconnected. In the last part of the book I will discuss ways to change your frequency short and long-term. Remember that the idea is transformation, not change. Forced change rarely works. Feeling better is the result of transformation.

**Thought for the day:** What kind of thoughts occur to you when you think that you are energy and made up of frequencies and everything you eat, drink, smell, feel, hear has a frequency? What if our eyes could see frequencies – what do you think the world would look like? Write down a list of as many items, activities, food, drink, and people that you encounter in a single day and guess their frequency. Which ones are high? Which ones are low? Now think about everything you did yesterday and guess the frequency. You may have no clue, try to do it intuitively. Your body knew exactly what was high and what was low frequency (I will also use the word vibration interchangeably) Include thoughts, words, people, food, drink, activities (T.V., etc.)

_____

_____

_____

_____

_____

_____

_____

_____

_____

_____

_____

_____

_____

_____

_____

_____

_____

_____

_____

_____

_____

_____

_____

# EXPERIMENTS OF DR. MASARU EMOTO

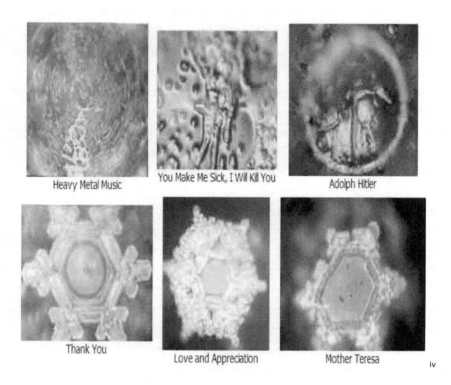

Heavy Metal Music

You Make Me Sick, I Will Kill You

Adolph Hitler

Thank You

Love and Appreciation

Mother Teresa

iv

14

Before          After

Effect on Water of Immune Vibration

500 people sending positive thoughts to bottled water

Prayer over Water

v

More interesting experiments by Dr. Emoto can be found online on sites such as: http://www.odditycentral.com/news/japanese-researcher-uses-controversial-experiments-to-prove-our-thoughts-and-intentions-can-alter-the-physical-world.html

# Day 4 - Quantum Physics Principle # 2
## *All energy vibrates on a frequency. Different things have different frequencies*

**Matthew 12:36** *says: "But I tell you, on the day of judgment men will have to give account for every* [a] *idle (inoperative, nonworking) word they speak."*

Frequencies have visible effects. Dr. Masaru Emoto did experiments on polluted water. He took vials of the same water and subjected them to different effects. Some had music played over them. Some had words written on the vials and some had words spoken over the vials. Then he quick-froze the water after a certain period of time and took samples and put under a microscope. The pictures you see on the previous two pages are the result. Dr. Masuru Emoto's experiments on water molecules resulted in several powerful conclusions:

1. Words and sound have the power to change water molecules
2. Thoughts have the power to change water molecules
3. The intention behind the words (i.e. love, hate) and music/sounds (Beethoven vs heavy metal) determines whether the effect is positive of negative.
4. Positive, high-frequency vibrations had a positive impact, negative, low-frequency vibrations had a negative impact.

Guess what? We are made up more than 60% water. Our thoughts, words and the sounds we give ear to have the power to change our DNA and molecules, as do the words and thoughts of others towards us. Here are other scriptures to consider:

**1 Peter 2:1:** *"So be done with every trace of wickedness (depravity, malignity) and all deceit and insincerity (pretense, hypocrisy) and grudges (envy, jealousy) and slander and evil speaking of every kind."*

**James 4:11-12:** *"Brethren, do not speak evil about or accuse one another. . . [But you] who are you that [you presume to] pass judgment on your neighbor?"*

**Thought for the day:** What kind of thoughts, sounds and words have you put before yourself today? If you were frozen water and you put a slice under on a slide under a microscope, what kind of picture would you see? Write down everything you have thought negatively about yourself yesterday and write down everything you thought about yourself positively. Do the same regarding other people. Date your page. Decide to try an experiment and for the next 3 days, focus on only thinking and saying positive things about yourself and positive things about other people. Use space below and end of book or your own journal.

_____

_____

_____

_____

_____

_____

_____

_____

_____

_____

_____

_____

_____

_____

_____

_____

_____

_____

_____

_____

_____

_____

_____

_____

_____

_____

# Day 5 - Quantum Physics Principle # 3
## Like Attracts Like

So we have established that we are made up of energy and that everything has a frequency. Negative things (low frequency) have negative impact and positive things (high frequency) have a positive impact.

This premise will be repeated on many levels throughout this journey. One of the main principles in Quantum Physics says that like frequencies attract like frequencies. This occurs in a magnetic type of fashion (although the science is quite complicated, all Quantum Physicists agree this is true). So high-frequency wave lengths attract high-frequency things and low-frequency wavelengths attracts low frequency things.

Emotions, thoughts, words, sounds, smells, all have frequencies and affect our body's overall frequency. Negative thoughts and emotions are low frequency in nature and attract negative things. If we have shame, anger, or fear, we tend to attract negative things into our life. If we are happy, joyful, peaceful and loving, we tend to attract good things into our life. By "things" I mean people, experiences, emotions, behaviors etc. Again, what matters is the overall vibration and is a cumulative effect. In other words, we could do some really good things to take care of ourselves health-wise but still be depressed and negative in our thinking. We often think if we try to forget painful things, they will go away but really they are just trapped inside and vibrating at a low frequency and therefore attracting more negative into our life. I will correlate this principle specifically with the concept of "faith" or "belief" to which Jesus refers repeatedly in the gospels.

**Matthew 9.29** says: *"Then he touched their eyes, saying, 'According to your faith, (and trust and reliance on the power in me) be it done to you,"*

**Thought for the day:** Let the idea of "like attracts like" sink in…meditate on this idea and let God begin to show you your life, experiences, beliefs, thoughts, feelings and how this principle has been true. This is the base principle for many of the correlating principles that will follow. Take a moment and reflect on chunks of time in your life like decades (0-10, 11-20 etc.) and think about what the overall vibration of that decade was for you as you recall experiences and memories (high or low). Don't forget to continue your assignment from Day 4.

_____
_____
_____
_____
_____
_____
_____
_____
_____
_____
_____
_____
_____
_____
_____
_____
_____
_____
_____
_____
_____
_____
_____
_____

# 3
# KNOW THE SUBCONSCIOUS
## DAYS 6-10

## *Day 6 – The Iceberg Principle*

***Proverbs 23:7:*** *"As a man thinks in his heart, so is he."*

O ver the years, psychologists have developed the principle of the subconscious. There is agreement that we are like an iceberg, only about 15% of what we know is in our conscious brain. Actually our brain can only hold so much at one time in working memory. Much of what we know (like how to tap our feet to the rhythm of a song or how to drink out of a glass) is in our implicit memory (we don't need to be thinking to do these things). Then there are our autonomic involuntary functions like blinking, breathing, etc. that happen without our awareness at all. The iceberg principle says that 85% of what we believe, feel and think lies in our sub (below the surface like an iceberg) conscious. This means that if we get reminded of this it can come to the surface. Some portion of our life is in our unconscious. We can't access it but as we make the subconscious conscious and release things, the unconscious moves to our subconscious) In other words, the more work we do on our thoughts, beliefs, feelings that are hidden, the more things will spontaneously arise that we have never been aware of before. In effect, the iceberg becomes smaller and more visible.

Did you know that we think more than 60,000 thoughts per day? So we are aware of about 9,000 of those 60,000. 51,000 thoughts or more per day escape our notice. They lie in our sub and unconscious. Remember the water experiments.

Some people might say our subconscious and unconscious is where our spirit lies. It knows everything about us like a supercomputer and is connected to God without our awareness of it.

**Thought for the day:** As you think about this iceberg principle, ask God to bring up something from your subconscious that you had forgotten. When this happens, what significance does this thing have in your life? Can you see where it has influenced you? Journal about this. This is your 3$^{rd}$ day to do the assignment from day 4. I challenge you to do it for another 3 days.

_____
_____
_____
_____
_____
_____
_____
_____
_____
_____
_____
_____
_____
_____
_____
_____
_____
_____
_____
_____
_____
_____
_____
_____
_____
_____
_____
_____
_____
_____

# Day 7 – Implicit Memories and Rituals

We develop beliefs based on experiences over the course of our life. Many beliefs are developed by watching our family behave repeatedly in the same manner (conditioning). One simple example of this is that my parents didn't profess to be practicing Christians but we prayed every night at dinner. You could call this a ritual. I never questioned this ritual. I just developed a belief that you were supposed to pray before dinner (not lunch or breakfast). I never thought about this belief or questioned why you only prayed at one meal a day. I'm not sure I ever questioned what the real purpose of prayer was except to acknowledge the existence of God. I'm not sure my parents did either. Families celebrate holidays with different traditions and rituals. Some family rituals are more dysfunctional like parents getting drunk every Thanksgiving or even every Friday PM and fighting. These repeated events that seem "normal" condition us to have beliefs about ourselves, others and the world. Many parents repeat what was taught to them to their children, passing on generational but destructive or negative (low-frequency) behaviors without ever really questioning them.

Because we accept what we have watched occur repeatedly, these beliefs become what we call implicit memories. We don't remember learning them, we just always remember we knew how to do it or it was a part of our life. These repeated experiences are one way that our beliefs are formed. This is repetition conditioning. Many people never question these rituals, they just accept them as true. Our brains are wired to think and do them. If we question them in realizing they are proprietary to our life experience (vs universal experience) then they become explicit and we choose what to do with these.

Realizing thoughts and beliefs are proprietary allows us to 1) Take personal ownership and; 2) Not judge others who don't agree or believe the same (i.e., if other people don't bless the food I don't think they are less spiritual)

**Proverbs 22:6:** *⁶Train up a child in the way he should go [and in keeping with his individual gift or bent], and when he is old he will not depart from it.*

**Thought for the Day:** Review your life and look at some family rituals. Did you think they were "normal" and "universal" in that everyone did these things? Write these down. Do you still believe and/or practice these? What is your opinion of these things? Based on Proverbs 22:6 – how well did your parents understand you and "train you up" in the way you were designed vs how much have you had to "unlearn"?

# *Day 8 – Implicit Memories, Dysfunction and Abuse*

The same concept we discussed yesterday holds true for dysfunctional and/or abusive behavior in a family. Every family has unspoken "rules". These are things that are allowed and not allowed in the family dynamic. One of the rules in my family was that there was no safety in talking about feelings. My parents' upbringing during the depression did not allow for emotions or feelings. So my highly empathetic gifts did not have a place to process. We call that a "no talk, no feel" rule. I could never share feelings and was not taught how to identify emotions as a young child. So I had no language for all the energy swirling inside of me. I developed the belief that you had to keep everything inside and figure out how to internally process and outside was a mask of "having it all together". There was not one traumatic event that caused that but a thousand ongoing cues that this was a family rule. This developmental handicap played a great role in my having an eating disorder as a teen and is a common, classic denominator in all addiction struggles.

Abusive parents often have belief systems that allow for them to cope with their abusive behavior towards their kids that also keep them from getting help (unless Child Protective Services intervenes). They pass these beliefs onto their kids. Some of these include: "It's your fault, you made me angry"; "This is how parents are supposed to discipline their children"; "If you weren't so irritating then I wouldn't have to hurt you"; and others. Generationally, these implicit beliefs get passed on because no one questions them or the coping mechanism of denial and rationalization allows them to perpetuate (shame is handed down generationally). Children learn to believe they are worthless, a burden, not loved, not valued, a possession, and exist for the pleasure of others (sexual). Also that marriage is unhappy. These beliefs are reinforced with repeated behaviors that may seem "normal" vs precise traumatic memories where the child knows something is wrong.

**Thought for the day:** Do you have any behaviors that you know are dysfunctional? See if you can track back to how those were rooted in beliefs that were accepted as normal in your family. Write these down. What kind of feelings are attached to these memories? Have you ever made a connection before between your struggle and the beliefs handed down to you? If your parents are still alive, can you have a conversation about this with them?

_____

_____

_____

_____

_____

_____

_____

_____

_____

_____

_____

_____

_____

_____

_____

_____

_____

_____

_____

_____

_____

_____

_____

_____

_____

_____

# Day 9 – Unprocessed, Negative Emotions

G ot the iceberg image in your mind? We live 85% of our life without awareness. Our perceptions of everything are dictated by these sub and unconscious beliefs and we are unaware that our views of everything are dictated by these beliefs. The negative beliefs are created during states of heightened negative emotions. The emotions are like mortar for the bricks of negative belief systems. Dr. Caroline Leaf talks about the brain neuronal systems looking like trees and structures.[vi] While our brain is only part of our belief system, these emotions locks the trees into place like dirt holding roots into the ground.

Based on Quantum Physics, negative emotions and beliefs vibrate at a low frequency. Imagine that you are a hot air balloon and negative, unprocessed emotions and beliefs are sandbags keeping the air balloon from soaring. Every time a sandbag is cut off then the air balloon goes a little higher. Remember the numerical frequency a couple of days ago? We started talking about things that raise and lower frequency. Negative emotions always lower frequency. Did you know that even the AMA now agrees that 80%+ of diseases are caused by negative emotions and beliefs? Remember the cumulative concept? Even if you are doing a lot of good high frequency things, the low frequency trapped emotions and beliefs are dragging down your overall vibration.

Negative emotions can get trapped in numerous ways. They are trapped in the first few years of life from the womb by absorbing intense emotions from parents because children are constantly by their side. Next they are trapped by our experiences in life where we don't have a place to process feelings or we don't even know we are feeling these things because the situations seem relatively normal. These experiences create beliefs (which can also be judgments which we'll talk about later). Traumatic events always result in trapped emotions because we cannot process them in the state of overwhelm or injury. We can also inherit negative emotions and beliefs. As Christians, we study the Bible for the purpose of *"renewing our mind."* (**Romans 12:2**) However, reading information does not convert the beliefs of our subconscious, especially those beliefs that are cemented with the mortar of trapped negative emotions.

**Thought for the day:** Subconscious beliefs creep into our mind in quietly arising thoughts. These beliefs don't align with what God says about us. They occur to us as true. Some might be: "Nothing goes my way", "No one will love me", and "I'll never get to have my heart's desire." "I am annoying", "I can't trust anybody". Pay attention to your thoughts today…what comes up when you listen intently to this? Write these down. If you did the exercise earlier, go back and look at some of the thoughts you wrote down. Do you see beliefs that these thoughts point to?

_____

_____

_____

_____

_____

_____

_____

_____

_____

_____

_____

_____

_____

_____

_____

_____

_____

_____

_____

_____

_____

_____

_____

_____

_____

# Day 10 – Triggers are Frequencies

***Ephesians 4:31*** *"Get rid of all bitterness, rage and anger, brawling and slander, along with every form of malice."*

Emotions have a frequency. Negative emotions vibrate on a low frequency and positive emotions on high frequency. (Anger, shame, guilt are low, love, joy and peace are high) When we have memories that are negative and we experience a situation similar to the one where the emotion was trapped, it acts like a tuning fork and causes that pain to awaken. We may call this a "trigger". It is actually two energies vibrating at the same frequency. The event will trigger the memory and the emotion at the same time. Often we don't recall the memory being triggered but feel the triggered feeling and conclude the event has the same familiar meaning and as the one we already created, thus reinforcing that this belief is in fact true. Like attracts like.

We cannot ignore emotions and think they will just go away. All unprocessed emotions are stored in our body as negative energy and they will affect our thoughts and how we view the world, ourselves and others. Again, low vibrations trapped in our body bring down our overall frequency and can affect our physical health (as earlier discussed) along with our emotional health. Ephesians 4 tells us that God is pure light and the gap between Him and us is widened by negative emotions, separating us and making us susceptible to evil. By getting rid of low vibration emotions we come closer to Him and more like Him. Our frequency goes higher and we come closer to pure light. Releasing negative emotions raises us up.

We truly are the result of our experiences and the beliefs we have created. We see the world through the lens created by the beliefs we formed by emotional experiences, our parents' influence and even beliefs in our DNA. In fact science is now proving that repeated thoughts get encoded on our DNA; so we do indeed pass our beliefs down to our children.

**Thought for the day:** Have you ever talked about the idea of "triggers." Is that a new concept to you? Think about a handful of events and separate the "what actually happened" (what you said, what they said, what they did, what you did etc.) from the "story" (what you thought it meant, how you felt, what you thought they intended or did deliberately, assumptions you made based on past experience.) Write this down – did you have any new understandings? Did you assign motive, and intent on the part of the other person as if you were in their head? Now dismantle it back to what actually happened and decide it means something else. Create a different meaning. How do you feel about it now?

---

# Day 11 – Subconscious Beliefs Dictate our Perceptions

*Colossians 3:8,* "*But now you must rid yourselves of all such things as these: anger, rage, malice, slander, and filthy language from your lips....*"

As I said, our perceptions occur to us as real truth. Here is an example. Someone says something to me and it hits a trapped emotion of rejection. (Triggers me) I don't necessarily remember the event that occurred to cause that emotion but I feel that feeling intensely and the belief or judgment about myself and/or the other person that was created during the triggered event gets brought up and occurs as a present experience. Therefore I project upon the other person that they have rejected me because this feels true. I may react in anger (masking hurt), get defensive, cry or withdraw based on my assumption. Remember, we don't actually know the intention of the other person unless we ask, but we assume we do because we feel a certain way. We project meaning as if it is objective truth.

When we are able to release the hidden negative emotions, identify the beliefs/judgments and then work on changing those (easier to tear down a wall with no mortar), then we don't get those low vibration/frequency negative emotions triggered any longer and get easily offended or hurt by others. It is difficult stay in joy when negative emotions are being triggered. Every time we change a belief, we diminish and eventually extinguish the connection of a type of event and the negative feeling related. Imagine a hot air balloon being weighted down by sandbags. It can't soar. As the sandbags are cut off/released, the balloon goes higher. We were meant to soar like that balloon. Hidden, low vibration, negative emotions keep us close to the ground. Releasing and forgiving the perceived offense brings true results.

**Thought for the day:** Like the exercise yesterday, think of an event that triggered you. Can you separate the "what happened" from the "meaning" you assigned? Think hard and see if you can connect it to a memory from your younger life when you felt that way. Write it down. Is it becoming easier to see how we add meaning, assumption, assign intent etc. in situations as if they are objectively true? Has someone ever done that to you where they assumed they knew your motive and what you "really" meant? Did it anger you for them to do that to you?

# 4
# KNOW THE LAWS AT WORK
## Days 12-20

## *Day 12 – The Law of Expansion*

*Job 3:25, "What I feared has come upon me; what I dreaded has happened to me."*

The Law of Expansion says that whatever you focus on you give energy to (thoughts are focused energy) and when you give energy to something it expands. We will talk about applications of this over the next few days. Remember the water molecule experiments of Dr. Emoto.

If we have hidden, negative emotions which are vibrating low and have helped create negative beliefs, what type of subconscious thought frequency do you suppose we are emitting, low or high vibration? If we are always afraid of things that might happen in the future as negative, we are focusing energy on fear and negative beliefs and causing them to be empowered and expand. Remember, like attracts like. This is especially true with fear. When we are in fear we focus on what we don't want to happen, it is automatic.

In the book of Job, it says Job lived his life in fear that bad things would happen and take away his prosperity. Then they did. From the Law of Expansion, Job was empowering the fear of loss and great loss occurred. (This does not negate the other truths in Job, just points out that fear opened the door for what happened)

As we move through all of these Laws, the basic core thought that we keep going back to is that we get what we believe we are going to get and these beliefs are mostly subconscious. Remember, like attracts like. If we women believe all men are cheaters, we will attract cheaters. If we believe things will be taken from us or that we won't really get what we want et al, that is exactly what will happen.

**Thought for the day:** Look back at some of your negative thoughts. Is there any correlation between those thoughts and things occurring repeatedly in your life? Do you walk around expecting for things to go wrong? (Is "Murphy" your middle name?) How much do you talk about expecting bad things, speaking negative things you believe about men, teenagers, girlfriends, bosses etc.? Maybe you think these things are universally true – are they true about you? Can you find exceptions (then not universally true) What if you really got everything you expected? What would you started "expecting" or what negative expectations would you want to change?

_____
_____
_____
_____
_____
_____
_____
_____
_____
_____
_____
_____
_____
_____
_____
_____
_____
_____
_____
_____
_____
_____
_____
_____
_____

# Day 13 – The Law of Expansion

*Mark 5:36: Jesus told him, "Don't be afraid; just believe."*

A s I stated, "you will get what you believe you will get." A fear-based paradigm has us focus on what we don't want. We mistakenly believe fear will help us prevent that thing from occurring. People do this every day but Quantum Physics says the opposite.

I am not afraid of my kids getting hurt. I was never hurt badly so I don't have a subconscious fear of it and I don't ever even think about it. Guess what? None of my kids have ever been in the ER. Now I'm not saying that is the only reason why, just that I do not think about them getting hurt ever, it just doesn't cross my mind. I could tell you many examples in people's lives of this same principle and the opposite; where in spite of hypervigilance, what they were afraid of happening comes to pass. I see these patterns occur all the time in my clients' lives and I hear the same from other practitioners and ministers. There are other principles like generational beliefs at work so it is not entirely our responsibility but uncovering all of our deepest fears is a good idea in this journey of life. Changing our beliefs and feelings are well worth the work involved.

Let me add an exception which is the Law of Grace. Remember that I said we get what we believe? We can become hyper-vigilant in the Law of Attraction also and this can cause fear that we are doomed if we have a bad day. I will talk about grace again. But if we believe that we can win if we practice being a little more than 50% positive over negative successfully, then we will. In other words, we don't have to fear screwing up either. That fear will also bring a belief system with it. (If I am not perfect, things will go wrong) Peace is resting in knowing the Laws and practicing them but it also lies in knowing we don't have to do it perfectly for it to work. Fear of mistakes can kick in this Law also. A quick, "oops" and getting our thoughts back on track goes a long way.

**Thought for the Day:** Sit quietly and ask your soul what are your
fears? Write them down. Can you trace them to events that
occurred or something you were conditioned to believe, even a
superstition? What bad things to you keep waiting to happen?
Would you like to not feel that fear?

_____

_____

_____

_____

_____

_____

_____

_____

_____

_____

_____

_____

_____

_____

_____

_____

_____

_____

_____

_____

_____

_____

_____

_____

_____

_____

_____

_____

_____

_____

# Day 14 – The Law of Sowing and Reaping

**Galatians 6:7,** "Do *not be deceived: God cannot be mocked. A man reaps what he sows.*"

Remember I said that the basic rule is that "you get what you believe". Another way to view this is a universal law, "You will reap what you sow". In The Law of Attraction they call this, "The Law of Reciprocity." We will get what we give in thought, word, and deed. Sow expectations, words, thoughts or deeds that are bad, and you will reap manifestations of bad. Sow expectations, words, thoughts, deeds that are good, and we will reap manifestations of good. Sow fear, reap negative events. Sow focused energy on positive, reap something positive. Give and you will receive. Give love, receive love, give hate, and receive hate. Give judgment and criticism, receive judgment and criticism. The Law of Reciprocity says, like Karma, I give and I get back.

The difference between these concepts and that of sowing and reaping is that in sowing and reaping, the reaping is always magnified. (Law of Expansion) We sow a seed and get a plant which contains many seeds. The growth process multiplies the seed into something greater. If we sow negative seeds (hate, criticism, cursing, judgment, anger, strife etc.) then negative roots, trees, plants, crops etc. will grow. When we sow good seeds, (love, joy, peace, gratitude, blessing) you get multiplied back many times what you sowed. Remember the water molecules. Sow positive, reap beautiful snowflakes; sow negative, reap ugly chaos/disorder. Whatever is truly residing in our subconscious will show because we do not control it. Many believe that since they aren't conscious of it, it doesn't affect them. This is not true, it still exists as negative trapped energy. The feelings, emotions and beliefs in our subconscious trump the beliefs in our conscious. We have to change them by releasing the energy behind them. This takes attention and effort but is doable.

**Thought for the day**: Think about the expanded ramifications of the principle of sowing and reaping. Write down some of the things in your life that comprise sowing, both good and bad. Have you seen reaping in this area yet? What has that looked like? Where could you possibly make some changes in giving? Can you eliminate some bad things you are sowing? Can you make space to add some positive things to sow?

_____

_____

_____

_____

_____

_____

_____

_____

_____

_____

_____

_____

_____

_____

_____

_____

_____

_____

_____

_____

_____

_____

_____

_____

_____

_____

# Day 15 – The Law of Sowing and Reaping
## Bitter Root Judgments

*Matthew 7:1*, *"Judge not lest you be judged, for the same measure you judge will be judged back upon you."*

This scripture means that however we judge someone or something, it will come back to us. It is another sowing and reaping process. We will either do the same things we judge or attract the same situation again (like attracts like) back to us. When we judge something or someone, we focus on it and give it power and so it expands. When we judge, we create an unconscious belief that then attracts reinforcement for that belief.

Jesus tells us that judging the heart of someone else is not our duty nor our right. Adam and Eve ate from the "tree of the knowledge of good and evil". Today we judge people based on what we think is good or evil in their heart. Jesus goes on to say in *v3*, *"Why do you look at the speck of sawdust in your brother's eye and pay no attention to the plank in your own eye? 4 How can you say to your brother, 'Let me take the speck out of your eye,' when all the time there is a plank in your own eye?"*

In the Law of Attraction, we get back what we give - the Law of Sowing and Reaping. If we give judgment, we get judgment back. What we judge in others will happen to us as well. How many times a day do we judge? A good sign of a judgment is the thought, "I would never do that." If we think that then there is a good indication we have judged. When we judge people and we don't repent, we pray negativity on them but we reap negativity back on us. Walking in love means we repent anytime we judge because it both sends negative energy to them and brings a negative consequence to us. Much of what occurs negatively is because we have judged...

**Thought for the day:** Begin to write down all the judgments you have made that come to mind. Most of us make multiple judgments a day. Imagine if every judgment you made today resulted in that thing coming back to you in the future. Would you be quick to repent? Be assured it will somehow. Let this motivate you to keep short accounts. Tomorrow I will walk through getting rid of the bitter root.

# Day 16 – The Law of Sowing and Reaping
## Bitter Root Judgments

**Matthew 7:5,** *"You hypocrite, first take the plank out of your own eye, and then you will see clearly to remove the speck from your brother's eye"*

Is your head reeling from realizing that we are judgment-making-machines? Yes we are. We are the sons of Adam constantly eating from the "tree of the knowledge of good and evil." We somehow believe we have been given the right to determine what's in people's hearts. When we really examine our own judgments and meaning and focus on removing those and are coming from a place of love, most often the judgments we have towards others disappear. Or when we determine that we are really thinking feeling or doing the same things we are judging others for doing then their "speck" seems so small. The process of negating judgments daily is a great way to stay clear of sending off low vibration negative signals to the universe to attract undesirable things. Like attracts like.

**Romans 2:1,** *"You, therefore, have no excuse, you who pass judgment on someone else, for at whatever point you judge the other, you are condemning yourself, because you who pass judgment do the same things. 2. Now we know that God's judgment against those who do such things is based on truth. 3So when you, a mere man, pass judgment on them and yet do the same things, do you think you will escape God's judgment?"*

So how do we undo this? We repent for making the judgment and often need to forgive the person we judged. If my boyfriend/girlfriend cheats on me and I judge them, I set up a belief that men/women to be untrustworthy. This is cemented in with feelings of betrayal. The Law of Bitter Root Judgments creates an attraction for this thing to find me again. If I forgive my boyfriend/girlfriend and repent for making the judgment then I negate and neutralize the negative energy I just sent out. Doing this process keeps me from creating the negative beliefs and locking them in with negative emotions.

**Thought for the Day:** Daily Practice: Recognize, repent, release, (forgive), restore (if it has caused broken relationship), redeem (what is God showing me about myself) and reprogram (what belief has been created that I don't like and what would I like to believe?)

_____

_____

_____

_____

_____

_____

_____

_____

_____

_____

_____

_____

_____

_____

_____

_____

_____

_____

_____

_____

_____

_____

_____

_____

_____

_____

_____

_____

_____

_____

# Day 17 – The Law of Sowing and Reaping Blessing

*Luke 6:28, 35, 37-38: 28 bless those who curse you, pray for those who mistreat you; 35 but love your enemies… Then your reward will be great… because He is kind to the ungrateful and wicked." 37 "Do not judge, and you will not be judged. Do not condemn, and you will not be condemned. Forgive, and you will be forgiven. 38 Give, and it will be given to you. A good measure, pressed down, shaken together and running over, will be poured into your lap. For with the measure you use, it will be measured to you."*

If we think of Bitter Root judgments as on a numerical frequency, when we judge we go from say a 300 to a -200. When we forgive we go to 0 and then repent brings us back to 300. In effect we have gained nothing, we have just eliminated reaping/attracting something negative, but have not attracted anything positive. To then decide to sow some good seeds we can go into the positive of 300 by blessing. Blessing is the word "barak" in Hebrew which means to "speak God's intention and to give something." God's intention is always positive. When we bless others, we sow a seed of positive intention and we can expect to see a harvest. If we stay at 300 we get no harvest, we have to move into the positive sowing to reap something good. We expand positive by focusing on it. "Give and it shall be given to you…." We have to give something – blessing is a powerful form of giving – it creates beautiful water crystals in others and we get back what we have given, multiplied.

This scripture in Luke repeats the message of Matthew 7. God loves everybody equally, even if they don't love Him. We are all flawed, we all have blind spots, and we are all on a journey of transformation. When we hate people, judge them or curse them, we get back what we give; God does not ever approve of this even if they did something unkind to us. When we bless those who have hurt us, the seed is even greater because it cost us something to forgive and bless. In the quote above, the verses in-between the ones quoted in Luke 6 say it's easy to bless someone who blesses us so it doesn't really reflect God's heart. Forgiving, repenting and blessing someone who has really wronged us is a major manifestation of the love of God and a seed that reaps a big harvest. God's ways are not our ways.

**Thought for the day:** How hard is it to bless someone that has hurt you? What about before they hurt you? When you weren't mad or bitter it was easier to speak a blessing. If you forgive them (and repent for judging) can you bless them now? Try it – it feels pretty good. Doesn't mean you have to trust them or be friends with them but you need to release them. Keep a journal of this. Make note if there was some kind of turn around or blessing in your life. Start tracking your judgments and blessings and see if you make connections in your life.

# Day 18 – Mindfulness of the Laws in Everyday Life

So by now you are thinking, "Oh I am just gonna hide out in my house and never interact with people so I don't keep sending out negative frequencies" But remember what I said earlier about fear and grace. So that doesn't really work either. No one said peace and joy are easy but they are possible. Here are a few tips on managing this successfully.

1.  Be present, in the moment in every conversation, be attuned to your preexisting judgments of that person.

The reality is that most of the time we are expecting and assuming the way another person will act based on judgments we have already made about them. For example, my friend is late for lunch and I am already mad because she is "always late" and I've judged her as inconsiderate. What if we intentionally stayed in place of blessing and looked instead for things to be affirming to the other person instead of judging faults? How would that affect the outcome?

2.  Stop several times a day, review your day and see if you have made judgments or been triggered and reacted. Ask, "Where did that come from?" Repent, forgive and bless that person.
3.  Take time each day to bless people you love and then people you may not really like (like a particular politician or someone you consider bad) pay attention to how different you feel.
4.  Remind yourself that God loves his children equally and does not play favorites or take sides. We are all connected so would you cut off your hand because you were mad at it?
5.  Pay attention to what you think and when you catch yourself in fear, worry or creating negative scenes, stop them mid-thought and create new ones.

**Remember**: We get what you believe so we ask ourselves in any situation, "What do I believe here?" What we give energy to expands, so give energy to solutions not problems and to positive rather than negative things. We reap what we sow so let's sow things we want to reap. Whatever we judge will be judged back on us so let's judge affirmatively.

**Thought for the day**: Think about all the relationships in your life. How much of your interaction with them is based on judgments you have already made about the "way they are" and how does this dominate your thoughts during any conversation. Imagine talking with them without any prior knowledge of them. How would your conversation change?

_____

_____

_____

_____

_____

_____

_____

_____

_____

_____

_____

_____

_____

_____

_____

_____

_____

_____

_____

_____

_____

_____

_____

_____

_____

_____

_____

_____

_____

# Day 19 – The Law of Grace and Mercy and the Science of Chaos

***Ephesians 2:8-9,*** *[8] For it is by free grace that you are saved (delivered from judgment...) through [your] faith (belief). And this is not of yourselves [ it came not through your own striving], but it is the gift of God; [9] Not because of works [not the fulfillment of the Law's demands], lest any man should boast. [Not the result of what anyone can possibly do, so no one can pride or glory to himself.]*

I said earlier that we can get into fear by obsessing over all the Laws at work. Remember frequency is cumulative and not about perfection. It is quantifiable. The Law of Grace and Mercy says that sometimes we get something we didn't earn. We don't deserve God's love and favor and sometimes people who we judge as undeserving still seem to get God's favor. But truthfully, we want the Law of Grace to be in existence because we don't want to get everything we deserve. More often than not , we have subconsciously sown some pretty negative frequencies. So if we put our belief in a God that loves us and wants us to have a joyful and peaceful life (remember we were wired for peace and joy) and believe that even if we make some mistakes, they can be undone, (forgiveness, repentance and blessing) then we can stay out of fear and legalism. Often most people don't truly believe God wants good for them. We tend to like laws but that's what ruined the Pharisees. So we don't want to substitute one version of legalism for another.

The Science of Chaos says that everything on the planet is interconnected but impossible to predict. The weather in New York City can be affected by a butterfly in the Rainforest. They cannot figure this out in Science, they just know it exists. God created this Science so His ways are even more intricately connected and beyond our comprehension. Grace trumps everything. We may see "divine coincidences" but never the whole picture. So all of this to say that in meditating on the laws and the correlating scripture, we want to always come down to believing that God is good and He loves us and His grace and mercy trump all of our mistakes. We want to believe that we can always ask for His grace and mercy. This will keep us out of fear that we have really so messed it up that the future is hopeless. We get what we believe.

**Thought for the Day:** Have you ever really thought about whether you believe that God is for you, that He wants you to be joyful and peaceful? Write down your thoughts with the opposite hand you normally write with. What does it say? Does it surprise you? Write down a belief about God that you would like to have. What does it say? What is keeping you from believing this about God?

_____

_____

_____

_____

_____

_____

_____

_____

_____

_____

_____

_____

_____

_____

_____

_____

_____

_____

_____

_____

_____

_____

_____

_____

_____

## *Day 20 – Review*

We are now two-thirds of the way through this journey. Take this day to go back and re-read parts of the last 20 days and spend a little more time journaling your thoughts.

My intention at this point is to have given you some tools to create intentional mindfulness using the laws explained, as well as starting to become aware of how you live your past in the present. Taking on a mindful way of life is the fundamental key to change moving forward. This stops the accumulation of negative emotions and beliefs. Addressing hidden subconscious emotions and beliefs will start cleaning up what is already there from your past. The last part of our journey will prepare you further to be mindful and give some more tips on raising your frequency in a variety of areas. Remember frequency is cumulative.

_____

_____

_____

_____

_____

_____

_____

_____

_____

_____

_____

_____

_____

_____

_____

_____

_____

_____

_____

# 5
# SHIFTING THE SOUL
## Days 21-26

### *Day 21 – Be a Pollyanna*

***Philippians 4:8-9*** ... [8]*whatever is true, whatever is honorable, whatever is right, whatever is pure, whatever is* [a]*lovely, whatever is of good repute, if there is any excellence and if anything worthy of praise,* [b]*dwell on these things* **9**... *practice these things, and the God of peace will be with you.."*

Paul is literally telling us to only think about positive things. Imagine paying attention to your thoughts 24/7 and whenever we catch yourself thinking anything negative, we shift your thinking to something positive. Most people would say that is unrealistic, Pollyannaish. Pollyanna was a literary character that was always positive. What if every single thought had a numerically identifiable frequency? Remember high-frequency thoughts attract favor, success, happiness peace, joy and love and low-frequency thoughts attract anger, fear, shame, humiliation, and hatred. Would you then reconsider the viability of Philippians 4:8? Do you think that Paul understood the LOA and that thinking on joyful, positive things would attractive joy and peace into your life? Don't you think the world was dark and heavy also during Paul's' time? If we watched TV during the Roman Empire, can we not imagine that the news would be probably worse than today's? What if positive thoughts vibrate at a 115 MHz and negative thoughts vibrate at a 25 MHz and our bodies are happy and healthy when we maintain a 68 MHz frequency? Could you see how we have the power to raise or lower our own vibration just by choosing conscious thoughts? Remember the Laws: Expansion, Reciprocity, Judgment and Grace? If Paul knew and understood these then he would be very deliberate about telling us to think on positive things. He repeats this throughout his letters in the New Testament.

**Thought for the day:** Write down 5 good things about several people including yourself and about your life. Then spend the day repeating these positive things in your head over and over again. Include people or situations that you normally don't think positively about. Do this for a couple days then write about how you feel and think after a couple of days of doing this. Again, if a bad thought pops in your head, pop it back out.

# Day 22 – What is your Heart?

*Proverbs 23:7,* "*As a man thinks in his heart, so is he.*"
*1 John 4:8,* "*He who does not love does not know God, because God is love.*"

**A**s a *Man Thinketh* was the title of one of the first LOA books written by James Allen in 1902. He based his book on the inferences of scripture although it was not a Christian book.

What is the heart? The Hebrew word in this scripture means the inner man or soul, maybe even the subconscious. It is making reference to judging in our inner man. The thoughts in our hearts are not seen by others and often not even ourselves, they are hidden.

Remember Dr. Emoto's water experiments. We are made up of 60% plus water. Our DNA is constantly being affected by our thought life. Our hearts carry the deepest places of belief. These places can even be unknown to ourselves. Did you know that the heart is up to 1000X more powerful than the brain electromagnetically and has almost as many memory cells? The hurts of life cause us to unconsciously put up walls around our heart to block love out and in… This wall disconnects us from others, the world and God.

When our deepest thoughts affect who we are and our life, wouldn't it be prudent to uncover as many of those thoughts as possible and reprogram the negative ones to positive? Wouldn't we want walls to come down and believe that we can be surrounded by safe people who love and support us? God did not intend for us to live with a fortress around our hearts that lock in negative emotions and beliefs creating isolation, mental and physical illness. Somewhere our experiences led us to put up these walls ourselves and we may have inherited beliefs about self-protection. Most people are not in touch with their heart or what it really wants. Most of us are driven by things we think we want but have never really identified the deep desires of our heart and asked for those.

**Thoughts for the Day**: Think about your heart and ask it what it wants…The answer may surprise you. How are you going about getting that? Ask your heart what is in the way. Can you identify bricks in a wall around your heart? What has caused those? What beliefs have those experiences created?

_____

_____

_____

_____

_____

_____

_____

_____

_____

_____

_____

_____

_____

_____

_____

_____

_____

_____

_____

_____

_____

_____

_____

_____

_____

_____

_____

_____

_____

_____

_____

# Day 23 – What do you Want?

***Matthew 6:21*** *"For where your treasure is, there is your heart also"*

J esus first talks about laying your treasures up in Heaven where they won't perish. He is referring to doing good, character, love, things that leave a wake of positive frequency. One of the principles of the LOA is about manifesting our desires. Being human implies we have many varied desires. Critics of the book *The Secret* believe the LOA is self-centered and about gratifying the flesh or worldly desires. But the paradox remains that God still loves us and wants to bless us. If we are indeed connected to Him, then the things our hearts treasure will relate to living a life of peace and joy.

Lack is a curse. While utter dependency on God requires great faith and this is pleasing to God, lack in general vibrates low. Choosing to avoid material possessions is a choice. Few people choose to starve or die of disease. But hedonism will never satisfy. A redeemed heart may like beautiful things but ultimately knows that things are illusory and if the cost of having them causes separation from God, then it-the heart doesn't really want them. A loving father gives good gifts to His kids.

When I question people deeply about what they really want, ultimately we get to a feeling and that what they want is what they think will produce that feeling (a mate, money, success etc.) Ultimately people want joy, peace, love….high frequency feelings and they want to feel connected to God and others. Again, when we take our thoughts captive and put high frequency thoughts in place, we move our frequency higher and are more likely to feel these feelings.

In the practice of the LOA, the thing we ask for is not always exactly what we get, often what we get is better. God's rewards are better. When we project our wants into the future we accept that we cannot have those good feelings today. This journey is about finding peace and joy where you are right now and it increasing in the future.

**Thoughts for the Day**: What things are you asking for? Why are you asking for those things? What will those things make you feel? Are those things the only way to get that feeling? Try to get down to the root of why you want what you want. When we ask for feelings rather than the vehicle that will create those feelings we often get something greater than the thing we asked for.

Ex. **I want to help people get healed.** Why?

**Because I will feel like I am here on earth to do something important.** What would that feel like?

**It would feel like I am special and chosen.** What does that feel like?

**It feels like unconditional love, it feels like value.** Is there any other way to feel that?

**Yes. I can feel that in communion with God.** So you don't need to help people in order to feel special? You can get that feeling right now?

**Yes. I feel special and I want to help people but I don't have to.**

_____

_____

_____

_____

_____

_____

_____

_____

_____

_____

_____

_____

_____

_____

_____

_____

# Day 24 – What do you Want?

***Romans 14:17*** *"For the kingdom of God is not eating and drinking, but* **righteousness**, **peace** *and* **joy** *in the Holy Spirit."*

***Luke 17:21,*** *". "...for behold, the Kingdom of God is within some of you."*[vii]

H ere is the very crux of why I want **everyone** to live in joy and peace. For years I thought the Kingdom of God was a place. The word Kingdom infers this. But how do we find this place? This scripture in Romans says that the Kingdom of God is a state of being. The LOA would call it a vibration or a frequency. Peace and joy, according to the Map of Consciousness created by Dr. David Hawkins[viii] are the highest frequency emotions. Jesus calibrates at 1000 (not MHz) (the highest frequency). ***1 John 4:8,*** says, *"God is love"* so *agape* love must also vibrate at 1000 along with the Holy Spirit. Peace and joy calibrate a little lower on this scale.

***Genesis 15:6*** says that *"Abram (Abraham) believed God and God credited it to him as righteousness".* This was before the law. Jesus fulfilled that law so our righteousness is rooted in our believing God (faith). Our righteousness is in the finished work of Christ and our adoption as sons, not in our works. Works leads to pride, shame, guilt, failure and other negative emotions that vibrate low. Having this faith always in our conscious frees us up to always be in a state of feeling loved unconditionally – the highest frequency.

So the Kingdom occurs when we are at a really high frequency. If Jesus, Agape and The Holy Spirit are/is the highest frequency, the closer we get to this, the more we experience the Kingdom of God, carry the intention of God for our lives and are able to impact others. Walking around negative and depressed and then confessing we are Christians is not a good sell for a relationship with Christ. High vibration people reflect God in their frequency.

**Thought for the Day:** We have established we give off a frequency. We have established that the Kingdom of God is a high frequency. Do you want people to see Christ in you? If so, then wouldn't you want to vibrate as close to the frequency of Jesus as possible? People are attracted to peace and joy. They are not attracted to depression, fear, shame, guilt etc. Often religion heaps these things on us for not measuring up. Can you see how opposite that is to what Jesus wants us to feel? How have you thought it was somehow righteous and Holy to feel these feelings? Did they make you feel closer to a loving God? Journal about this and what negative, low frequency emotions you want to shed.

_____

_____

_____

_____

_____

_____

_____

_____

_____

_____

_____

_____

_____

_____

_____

_____

_____

_____

_____

_____

_____

_____

_____

_____

# Day 25 – The Real Secret

*Matthew 6:33, "Seek first the Kingdom of God and all these things will be added to you."*

Earlier in Matthew 6 we see that "all these things" means abundant provision. If we substitute from yesterday's lesson here we get, "Seek first Faith/Trust in God's love, peace and joy and provision will always be there." This now takes on a different meaning.[ix] If we make staying at faith/trust, love, peace and joy our priority, we will stay at a high vibration and always be attracting like (good) things. We know that faith/trust, love, peace and joy will only truly come when our relationship with God is our first priority. A troubled conscience will always interfere with peace. Imagine if you suddenly realized that worrying about finances was the very thing that was keeping provision from manifesting. Worry (fear) is the opposite of love and a very low frequency. There are several applications of the LOA here. "Like attracts like" – worry – low frequency attracts negative things, i.e., poverty, failure, loss. The law of expansion – focusing on lack expands lack. Focusing on love, peace and joy expands to bring more and "all these things."

This lesson is key to changing your thinking. We have to intentionally shift from worry and fear. It is not easy because our brain is attempting to get back to joy and peace. Problem solving or fixing/controlling has been the way the ruts in our brain have formed, so we have to create new neural pathways deliberately. If we defer to God in this state and stop trying to "figure it out," we can trust that He will make a way. This does not condone inactivity or laziness, only that striving in our own efforts will not bring us what we want. Worry and striving will always be counter to peace and joy. Remember we get what we believe. I hope that you have "drunk the Kool-Aid" at this point because this only works if we change our frequency and believe/trust that we will get what you believe.

**Thought for the Day:** At this point in the journey, have you really bought into the message? If not, what has been the obstacle? Write that down. Can you do some troubleshooting to overcome that obstacle? It may be rooted in trapped emotions and beliefs. This message is not unique to me. Look for other reinforcements if necessary. Find the way to begin to let go of worry. Even just a little will bring changes about. Sometimes a snowball effect occurs when you can change just a little bit.

_____
_____
_____
_____
_____
_____
_____
_____
_____
_____
_____
_____
_____
_____
_____
_____
_____
_____
_____
_____
_____
_____
_____
_____
_____

# Day 26: Icing on the Cake - Gratitude

*Philippians 4:6, "Do not be anxious about anything, but in every situation, by prayer and petition, with thanksgiving, present your requests to God."*

Gratitude is another high-vibration action and attitude. *1 Thessalonians 5:18, "Give thanks in all circumstances; for this is God's will for you in Christ Jesus."* Gratitude is big part of the Kingdom. It is a state that immediately shifts our minds from negative to positive  Remember we get what we focus upon (expansion) so if we focus on things as abundant (what we have) and not our lack (what we don't have) we expand what we have. Gratitude vibrates high and this is God's will for us – like peace and joy. Throughout scripture we are encouraged to give thanks to God. Gratitude changes and shifts things. God is not hiding. He wants to give us clues to how to be connected to him. Philippians 4:6 demonstrates that faith, (the same as righteousness in *Romans 14:17*) joy (abiding, connected and surrendered to God); and gratitude leads to answered prayer what we want (our requests to God).

So, in a nutshell, getting what we ask/pray for has to do with being connected to (abiding) God in joy, peace, faith and gratitude; not in fear, anxiety, doubt, control and lack. Many scriptures reiterate this truth. High-vibration states elicit the things we want from God. In effect, He better hears us when we are vibrating high. (It seems sometimes He still answers in our desperate whiny prayers) but repeatedly we are encouraged to stay in positive states if we want to have God's ear. This aligns with all of the LOA principles discussed in the past weeks. When we are thankful, we get more things to be thankful for. (Laws of Expansion, Sowing and Reaping) Fathers want to give good gifts to their children but they are especially delighted when their children are grateful and not entitled. Remember, the secret to everything weighs primarily on our thought life and the feelings attached. So focus on what makes us feel great. Gratitude is a tool to quickly shift our frequency.

**Thought for the Day:** Stop right now and think of 10 things you are grateful for. Say them out loud. Do you notice that you feel differently? Write down 20 things you are grateful for. Think about what is missing in your life. How much time do you focus on what is missing versus what you have? Write down percentages of time. What can you do to shift this percentage to weigh more heavily in gratitude?

# 6
# OTHER WAYS TO RAISE FREQUENCY
## Days 27-30

### Day 27 - You are what you eat (vibrationally)

Yes, there it is. I know some of you were dreading this topic. Well the good news is I am not going to give you a diet plan, or talk about anything about what you should or shouldn't do, or shame you in any way. That is not the way a high vibration person thinks and acts. Most people "should" all over themselves their entire life. This vibrates very low; it's the sign of a prisoner. When we shift our attitude towards what we "get" to do versus what we "have" to do; our frequency raises. We choose our life every minute of every day. Choosing vibrates high, "Have to", "ought to" and "should" vibrate low. Get it?

Many people don't connect what they eat and how they feel because they see eating healthily as a "should". Let me propose a shift in our thinking about food. Remember, our frequency is cumulative. Food also calibrates at high and low numbers. So putting high frequency foods in our body raises our vibration and we feel better. Like attracts like. I would say that if we want financial abundance, eat healthy. If we want love, eat healthy. If we want physical health, eat healthy. They are all connected. This is not about losing weight at all. The higher our frequency, the more likely we are to attract what we really want and be at peace and joy. (And the reverse is also true) So we can see the connection with food and peace and joy but our brain/attitude has to also embrace this joyfully or the negative thinking will counteract the positive food. Comfort foods often medicate us in the moment but long-term they lower our frequency, especially alcohol, drugs and white refined sugar. (Which is not anything close to its original chemical state) These are particularly so because they alter our brain chemistry initially, but then leave our chemistry in a deficit state. So the result is a depletion in the neurotransmitters that help us feel happy and think positive thoughts. (They add to depression and anxiety) Oh and don't forget water …half your body weight in ounces per day.

**Thought for the day:** Start looking at food in a numerical frequency manner. Raw, fresh, organic, = high; canned, processed, overcooked, = low. Think about a couple of things you like that vibrate high and add them to your regular regimen of foods. Begin to think about some low frequency things you can eliminate.

# Day 28 - Absorbing Positive and Negative Energy

People flippantly make comments like, "I got a bad vibe there," or "Wow, I really felt positive/good energy there." It seems though, in general, few people really pay close attention to the energy around them. I believe that so few people ever feel really good for a consistent period or experience real peace and joy that they are desensitized. It is said that the higher your vibration is, the more aware you become of the frequency of your surroundings. This certainly has been true in my life. Remember, frequency is cumulative and we can absorb the energy from other people, places, and things. What we hear, see, smell, taste (like in yesterday's lesson) and touch also can affect our frequency. If we begin to view everything in terms of measurable/calibratable frequencies, we can truly get a picture of exactly how responsible we are for our lives and vibrations. Then we can make choices that result in staying at a high-frequency. What is peace and joy worth to you?

Negative people give off low-frequency vibrations in word and deed. We get to decide who we "hang out" with. If someone is depressed and we are comforting or trying to minister to them, this is different than just letting them suck the life out of us. Positive people give life to everyone around them. T.V. shows, movies, etc. add or subtract as does music (remember the water experiments). The news typically vibrates low along with movies about horror, death, evil etc. Good feeling T.V. shows, inspirational movies, Worship, prayer and connecting to God vibrates high. Laughing, exercising, having fun, doing things we enjoy and are fulfilling raise vibration. Loving our work and choosing to have a passion for it raises our vibration. Essential oils vibrate higher than many other things and using them raises our vibration. Good quality nutritional supplements raise our vibration. Being in nature (nature vibrates high, live vibrates higher than dead) raises our vibration. Opening our heart and giving and receiving love and heart energy raises our vibration. Getting enough rest maintains our vibration. Electromagnetic frequency from T.V., microwaves, computers, phones etc. lowers vibration. Subluxations lower vibration. Blockages in the body's energy and electrical systems, toxicity also lower vibration. Stress lowers vibration. Everything is quantifiable.

**Thought for the Day:** Review the last 7 days of your life and write down everything you remember doing and decide if it was an addition to your cumulative frequency calibration or a subtraction. What did you notice? Can you correlate feelings or behaviors that occur after high-frequency things on your list? Can you do the same with low-frequency things on your list?

_____

_____

_____

_____

_____

_____

_____

_____

_____

_____

_____

_____

_____

_____

_____

_____

_____

_____

_____

_____

_____

_____

_____

_____

_____

_____

_____

_____

_____

_____

# Day 29- Live Like a Son (Not a slave)

*Galatians 4:6,* "*and because you are sons, God sent out the Spirit of his Son into our hearts, crying out, "Abba!*[b] *(Father!)," *[7]* so that you are no longer a slave but a son, and if a son, also an heir through God.*"

Imagine your father is the greatest, wealthiest king on the planet. Imagine that you are a prince/princess raised in the palace all your life. Imagine everything he owns is also yours. Imagine that you have the authority that he carries. Imagine he loved you with an incredible, unconditional love. How would you see and live life if this were true? Galatians 4 tells us that this true. Yet most of us live life as if we are slaves. A slave is always expecting negative, bad things to happen. A slave lives with ought to, should, have to mentality. A slave never expects more than what they can see. A slave has limits because they don't "deserve" God's favor or blessings. A slave serves out of duty and obligation. A slave vibrates low, and does not usually experience peace and joy.

If we did not have a loving father, it becomes difficult to embrace God in our heart/subconscious as a loving father. We live in a performance-based society where love is earned. We project that upon our God, even in the church. In spite of what Jesus has done on the cross, we keep trying to earn the right to be loved by God or have His favor so we keep getting what we expect. Do you think a prince believes that life won't go his way? No, he believes he carries a powerful voice and authority to carve his destiny. He never imagines himself helpless or powerless. He is at peace that all of his needs are taken care of and goes about doing his father's business. He serves out of love, out of belief His father has the best plan for his life. He serves cheerfully because he chooses to. He lives his life by choice not duty or obligation. Princes vibrate high.

When we shift to believe that God, the universe, life, etc. are for us instead of against us, we sow a new seed (Remember this law?) and expect for positive things to happen on an unconscious level. When we truly eliminate a slavery mentality, we will begin to see the manifestation of the things a prince/heir/son expects to see in their life: fruit, abundance, power, authority, purpose, and destiny. ...

**Thought for the Day:** Look at all the areas of your life: family, marriage/relationship, friends, work, money, health, fun, spirituality. In what areas have you been behaving like a slave: expecting bad things to happen and that the world was against you? In what areas have you believed you had favor? How do each of those areas manifest what you believed about them? Write down a plan to believe something different that reflects sonship not slavery in the areas that have not gone well for you. Create a list of "I am" statements that reflect sonship (I am made in his image) for example: I am beautiful, I am smart, I am successful, I am loved/lovable, I am safe, I am powerful, and I am here for a purpose....

_____

_____

_____

_____

_____

_____

_____

_____

_____

_____

_____

_____

_____

_____

_____

_____

_____

_____

_____

_____

_____

_____

_____

_____

# Day 30 – Wrapping it all up

*1 Corinthians 10:23*, *""I have the right to do anything," you say--but not everything is beneficial." I have the right to do anything"--but not everything is constructive."*

I have repeatedly said that frequency is cumulative. In my practice as an Emotion Code Practitioner I find that the main root of almost everything goes back to trapped negative emotions and the corresponding negative beliefs. Even the AMA is in agreement that this is true. So the idea is to practice everything we have learned but our emotions and thoughts trump all of the rest. Here is a quick review of things to apply to your life daily.

- Forgive, repent and bless several times a day or as you catch yourself judging someone (Law of Sowing and Reaping)
- Learn and implement ways to quickly process negative emotions when they arise. (Don't let the sun go down on your anger)
- Work to access past hidden negative emotions and beliefs and reprogram them. (You can find an Emotion Code Practitioner, a therapist or some other practitioner who helps access that which is hidden)
- Intentionally sow good seeds in word, thought, and deed (Law of Expansion) for yourself too.
- When you catch yourself thinking negative thoughts, change them. Like attracts like (fear begets fear etc.)
- Don't treat this work like "I have to do it perfectly or bad things will happen." (fear) Remember the Law of Grace (you get what you believe so believe that if you do a little bit, you will get great results)
- Eat good food, avoid bad, drink water, rest, exercise, play, laugh, get in nature, surrender control, use oils and supplements
- Pay attention to what goes into your eyes, ears, mouth and nose.
- Pay attention to who you are surrounding yourself with and the energy you are absorbing from them or they are taking from you.

**Thought for the Day:** Now is where the rubber meets the road. What will you do from here on out? Will you forget all the hard work you have done for the past 29 days? Will you just let your brain resume its ways? It takes reinforcement for neuronal pathways in the brain to change permanently. We have uprooted a bunch of old trees in your brain (that's what neuronal systems look like) and planted some new ones but they need watering. Journal about your thoughts.

_____

_____

_____

_____

_____

_____

_____

_____

_____

_____

_____

_____

_____

_____

_____

_____

_____

_____

_____

_____

_____

_____

_____

_____

_____

_____

_____

_____

_____

# Daily Checklist
## (First thing in Am and last thing in PM)

**This will take about 10-20 minutes each am but it will change your life and you will find things go much better overall in every area of your life.**

**AM** – Today I will...

\_\_\_\_ Do my list of affirmations today (I am statements – Day 29)

\_\_\_\_ Bless 5-10 people this am (speak it out loud) (Day 17)

\_\_\_\_ Reach out to 1+ people today to encourage and affirm. (Day 4, 14)

\_\_\_\_ Commit to pay attention to my thoughts and words today and When I catch myself thinking or speaking negatively, stop it, repent, forgive and bless if appropriate (Day 18)

\_\_\_\_ Choose to put high frequency food and water in my body (Day 27)

\_\_\_\_ Choose something different about what I watch or do (Day 28)

\_\_\_\_ Set boundaries with negative people or just avoid them (Day 28)

\_\_\_\_ Stop and enjoy the moment (smell the roses) today (Day 29)

\_\_\_\_ State 5-10 things I are grateful for (Day 26)

\_\_\_\_ Spend 5+ minutes imagining what I want today and future – be specific and say out loud what I am imagining (Day 13)

\_\_\_\_ (Add your own) _____

# PM

___ Did I forgive, repent and bless?  Do it now (Day 16)

___ Did I bless 5-10 people?  Do it now (Day 17)

___ Did I express gratitude for 5-10 things?  Do it now (Day 26)

___ Did I think negative thoughts towards myself? Do "I Am" now
(Day 29)

___ Think only positive things right now for 5-10 minutes (Day 21)

___ Did I absorb negative energy today?
     Think about it leaving your body right now. (Day 28)

___ Did I run my day like a son or a slave? (Day 29)

___ Did I notice any unconscious beliefs creeping up from my
subconscious?  (Day 9)
___ Did I pay attention to what happened versus what I made it
mean today? (Day 10)
___ Did I decide to challenge and change those beliefs? (Day 11)

___ (Add your own)

# JOURNAL PAGES

You can journal your daily answers here or use a
separate journal, whatever you want to do.

## Day 1

_____
_____
_____
_____
_____
_____
_____
_____
_____
_____
_____
_____
_____
_____
_____
_____
_____
_____
_____
_____
_____
_____
_____
_____
_____
_____
_____
_____
_____
_____
_____
_____
_____

# Day 2

# Day 3

# Day 4

# Day 5

# Day 6

# Day 7

# Day 8

# Day 9

# Day 10

# Day 11

# Day 12

# Day 13

# Day 14

# Day 15

# Day 16

# Day 17

# Day 18

# Day 19

# Day 20

# Day 21

# Day 21

# Day 22

# Day 23

# Day 24

# Day 25

# Day 26

# Day 27

# Day 28

# Day 29

# Day 30

# ABOUT THE AUTHOR

Robin Perry Braun, MPsy is the President of Integrated Life Strategies, Inc. She serves her clients primarily using energy techniques combined with years of education and experience in prayer ministry and various counseling models. Her eclectic background gives her a full toolbox. Her passion is to bring people into freedom and help empower them to live full lives in body, soul and spirit. Ultimately she believes to achieve our destiny we must live in a state of thrival and high vibration. She also teaches workshops, seminars and classes and works with corporate and church leadership to bring her model of corporate attraction to manifestation.

You can find out more about consulting and/or contracting with Robin via her website: www.Integratedlifestrategies.com

---

[i] From Kay Warren, Choose Joy because Happiness isn't Enough (Revell, Grand Rapids, MI) 2012

[ii] Allan N. Schore, M.D., *Affect Regulation the Origin of Self: The neurobiology of Emotional Development* (Hillsborough, NJ, Lawrence Erlbaum Associates, Inc.) 1994

[iii] http://cellphonesafety.wordpress.com/2006/09/17/the-frequency-of-the-human-bodyand-your-coffee/

[iv] http://www.fengshuidana.com/2012/11/13/the-intense-power-of-your-thoughts-words-environments/

[v] http://www.pinterest.com/deniseddmartin/water-crystals/

[vi] http://drleaf.com/blog/thoughts-are-real/

[vii] Some of this concept from Dr. George Burriss, II, Ph.D., Munger Place Church, Dallas, TX

[viii] David R Hawkins, M.D., Ph.D., Power Vs Force (Carlsbad, CA: Hay House, Inc.) 1995, 1998, 2002, 2012

[ix] Per Dr. George Burriss

Made in the USA
Middletown, DE
04 June 2024